better together*

*This book is best read together, grownup and kid.

 akidsco.com

a
kids
book
about

a kids book about

coping skills

by Megan Knipe

A Kids Co.
Editor Emma Wolf
Designer Rick DeLucco
Creative Director Rick DeLucco
Studio Manager Kenya Feldes
Sales Director Melanie Wilkins
Head of Books Jennifer Goldstein
CEO and Founder Jelani Memory

DK
Editor Emma Roberts
Senior Production Editor Jennifer Murray
Senior Production Controller Louise Minihane
Senior Acquisitions Editor Katy Flint
Acquisitions Project Editor Sara Forster
Managing Art Editor Vicky Short
Publishing Director Mark Searle
DK would like to thank Natasha Devon

First published in Great Britain in 2025 by
Dorling Kindersley Limited
20 Vauxhall Bridge Road,
London SW1V 2SA
A Penguin Random House Company

The authorised representative in the EEA is
Dorling Kindersley Verlag GmbH. Arnulfstr. 124, 80636 Munich, Germany

A CIP catalogue record for this book is available from the British Library.

ISBN: 978-0-2417-2596-2

Printed and bound in China

www.dk.com

akidsco.com

MIX
Paper | Supporting
responsible forestry
FSC™ C018179

This book was made with Forest
Stewardship Council™ certified
paper – one small step in DK's
commitment to a sustainable future.
Learn more at **www.dk.com/uk/
information/sustainability**

To my husband, Rich; thank you for believing in me. And to our boys, Edwin and Domenic. I love each of you endlessly!

Intro
for grownups

You may be wondering why it's necessary to talk about coping skills with kids. Well, the reality is that we all use coping skills each and every day! When our body sends signals to our brain, we react. The goal of this book is to encourage kids to pause and plan out which response will be most healthy and productive instead of reacting with their first urge (which can often be harmful or inappropriate).

Every parent or caregiver likely knows what it's like to encourage their kids to, "Stop hitting!", "Calm down!", or, "Stop screaming!". These are negative coping skills. But what if instead of shutting down inappropriate reactions, we start teaching positive responses long before a tough situation arises? This way, our kids can be prepared to pause and respond thoughtfully and, in turn, begin a long and beautiful journey of creating healthy and impactful relationships with themselves and others.

Hi! My name is Megan.

I'm a mum to 2 sons, and I know a lot about how kids think, play, and learn.

I'm excited to talk to you about coping skills today!

I want my kids (and kids like you)
to have a book that can help them
start this important conversation.

Let's dive in!

So, what are **coping skills?**

Coping skills are actions or thoughts we use in response to big feelings.

For example, I want you to think about a time you felt angry.

Like, *really* angry.

What was the first thing
your body wanted to do?

Yell really loud at your grownups?

Hit the closest thing to you?

Both of those responses feel natural, but they aren't the healthiest coping skills.

Many times, the first thing we want to do isn't the best way of dealing with our big feelings.

Now, I'm not saying there's an issue with feeling anger.

It's normal!

Those big feelings are nothing to feel ashamed of; we all experience them.

But, how can we choose to respond to feelings in a way that's **helpful** instead of **harmful** to us or others?

Instead of immediately reacting, try... pa

using...

Take a moment to think, and take a deep breath while you're at it.

Now you have some time to try and understand your big feelings and think about what's best to do next.

So, what *can* you do next?

You can...

+ talk about what's bothering you with someone you trust.

+ ask for space (maybe have some alone time in your room).

+ ask for a hug.

+ scream into a pillow.

+ listen to your favourite song.

+ ball up your fists.

+ play with a fidget toy.

And lots of other things work, too.

These are all examples
of healthy coping skills.

What do you think would help **YOU** the most when you're experiencing big feelings?

When we choose healthy coping skills, we treat ourselves and our feelings with respect.

We recognize that our feelings deserve to be felt, but we can choose to react to them in a way that's safe for us and those around us.

The truth is, a lot of people I know (myself included) don't learn these kinds of skills until they're grownups. (And they really wish they'd figured them out sooner!)

I believe developing coping skills as a kid is one of the most powerful things you can do for your lifelong health.

So, wa
You're learning so

y to go!

me important stuff!

Building a toolkit of coping skills now will help you work through big feelings for the rest of your life.

And it'll give you lots of healthy responses to choose from when you feel different kinds of feelings.

Nobody feels 100% great all of the time. Right?

And when our bodies aren't operating at their best, it can affect how we feel and think.

For me, when I start to get hungry,
I also start to feel super grumpy.

Now that I know that about myself, I can be prepared with a snack when I start to feel hungry to keep myself from getting grumpy. **That's a coping skill!**

Our bodies are always communicating with us.

And it's important to learn what our bodies are telling us so we can respond in a way that's helpful.

As you grow, yo
and grow

ur needs change with you.

So it's important and respond to ways as you co into new ver

to keep learning
your body in new
ntinue to grow
sions of you.

The coping skills

different from now as a

I used as a kid are

those I use grownup!

Growing and changing

 can be really uncomfortable.

But embracing those changes and learning how to respond to your body's needs in a healthy way is an awesome way to love yourself!

We can't control what others do and say around us, but we can control...

how we
respond and
how we treat
ourselves.

So, keep learning, have patience and take it

keep growing, with yourself, one day at a time.

I believe

in you!

Outro
for grownups

Creating a toolkit full of healthy coping skills doesn't happen overnight. It takes time and practice! Progress not perfection. As long as we keep trying to learn, grow, and be the best we can be, we're helping our mind and body to be as healthy as possible. This is good for us *and* the world around us!

Coping skills look different for everyone, and what works for the kid you're reading with today may not work for them a month from now, or a year from now. Encourage them to keep exploring their feelings and talking about what skills are and aren't working for them.

The first example of what coping skills are comes directly from us, the grownups, to the kids in our lives! Actions speak far louder than words. What coping skills do you use?

About The Author

Megan Knipe wrote this book for her sons – and for all kids! She first discovered the importance of developing healthy coping skills as a young adult. After struggling with drug and alcohol addiction, she found an entirely new way of life within sobriety and began her journey of discovering the importance of setting boundaries, utilizing healthy coping skills, and creating a life that she genuinely loves.

She graduated from Liberty University with a bachelor's degree in early childhood education and later with an MA in counselling. One day, she hopes to work in the counselling field, but for now she stays at home with her 2 sons, Edwin and Domenic. She currently works from home as an online business manager for Allison Jandu from the Potty Training Consultant, helping families work through big transitions.

Megan is incredibly grateful for her family, counsellors, mentors, and dear friends who have stood by her, watched her grow, and continue to support her.

 @meganknipe_   @raising.cyclebreakers   @megan-knipe

Made to empower.

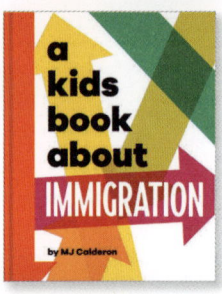

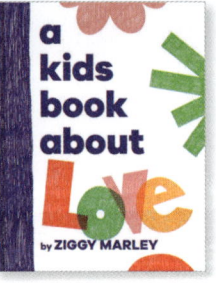
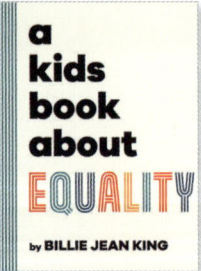

Discover more at akidsco.com